The Baroque Story

Author & Illustrator
Gisel A. Costa

Copyright © 2015, 2019 Gisel A Costa. All rights reserved.
No part of this book may be reproduced or copied in any form
without written permission from the copyright owner.
For information regarding permission kindly email:

TheErasTheBaroqueStory@gmail.com

Zoe and Isabella are home and getting ready for their music recital.

Their brother David and his friends Mark and Zachary are gathering their brushes for their art lesson.

Zoe said, "Isabella, remember Ms. Gisel said we need to practice to be comfortable when we perform. She also assigned page 39 in the book. Come to the piano and I will be your teacher today".

Isabella followed her sister to the piano
and opened her book to page 39.
They noticed another book there too.
Isabella said,
"Oh that's the story Ms. Gisel read to us!
Read it Teacher Zoe -"
"What is the name of the piece?" Zoe asked.
"Minuet in G by Bach" Isabella answered.

"Can you read the story Ms. Gisel read the other day please?" Isabella asked.

"Yeah!" Zoe said.

"She left her Baroque history book here! She also said back in the day these guys practiced and wrote these pieces! I want to write a song one day too. So practice can definitely help."

Zoe grabbed the book and began to read:

Instead of lamps, there were candles.

Instead of pianos, there were harpsichords.

This time was known as the Baroque Period. Baroque means "imperfect pearl".

There were a group of boys named **Bach, Vivaldi,** and **Handel** during this time.

They played their own instruments and they went to their music lessons.

They wrote their own music too so they were known as composers.

Bach played the violin, harpsichord, and organ in huge churches.

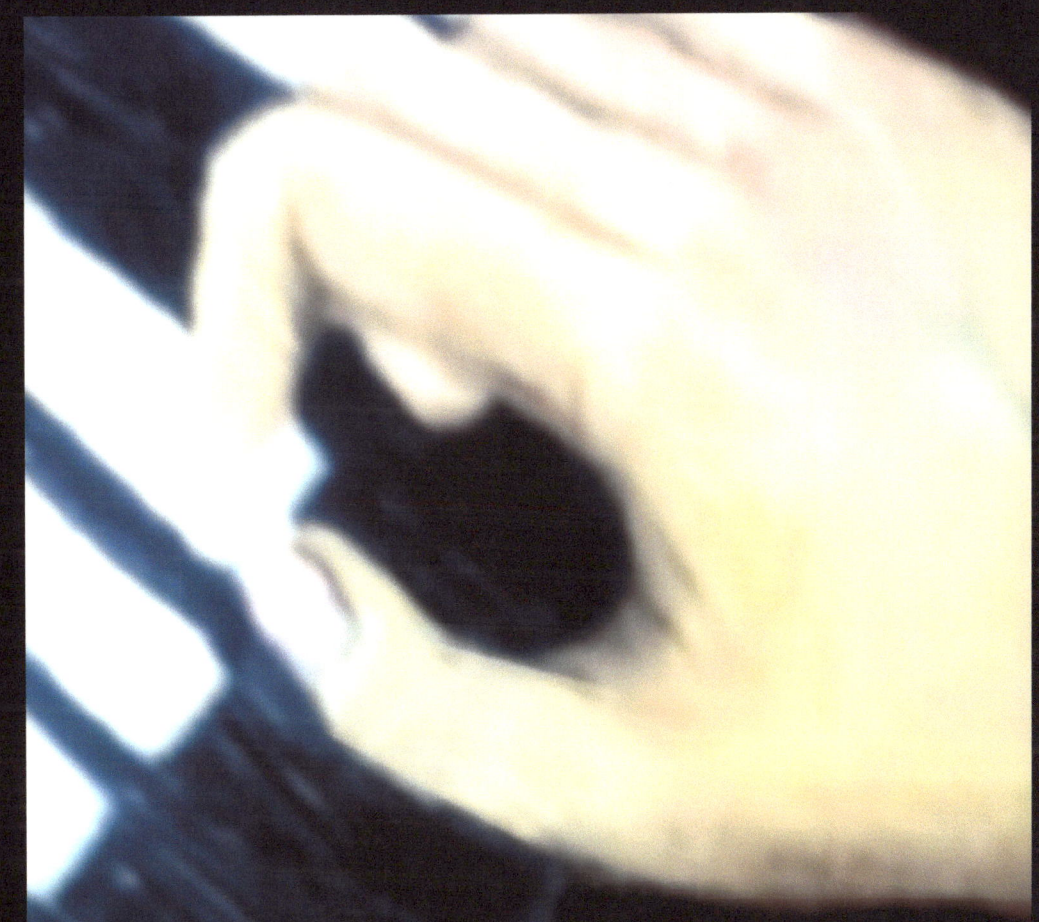

He wrote over
1000 compositions,
and he practiced every day.

Vivaldi played the violin.

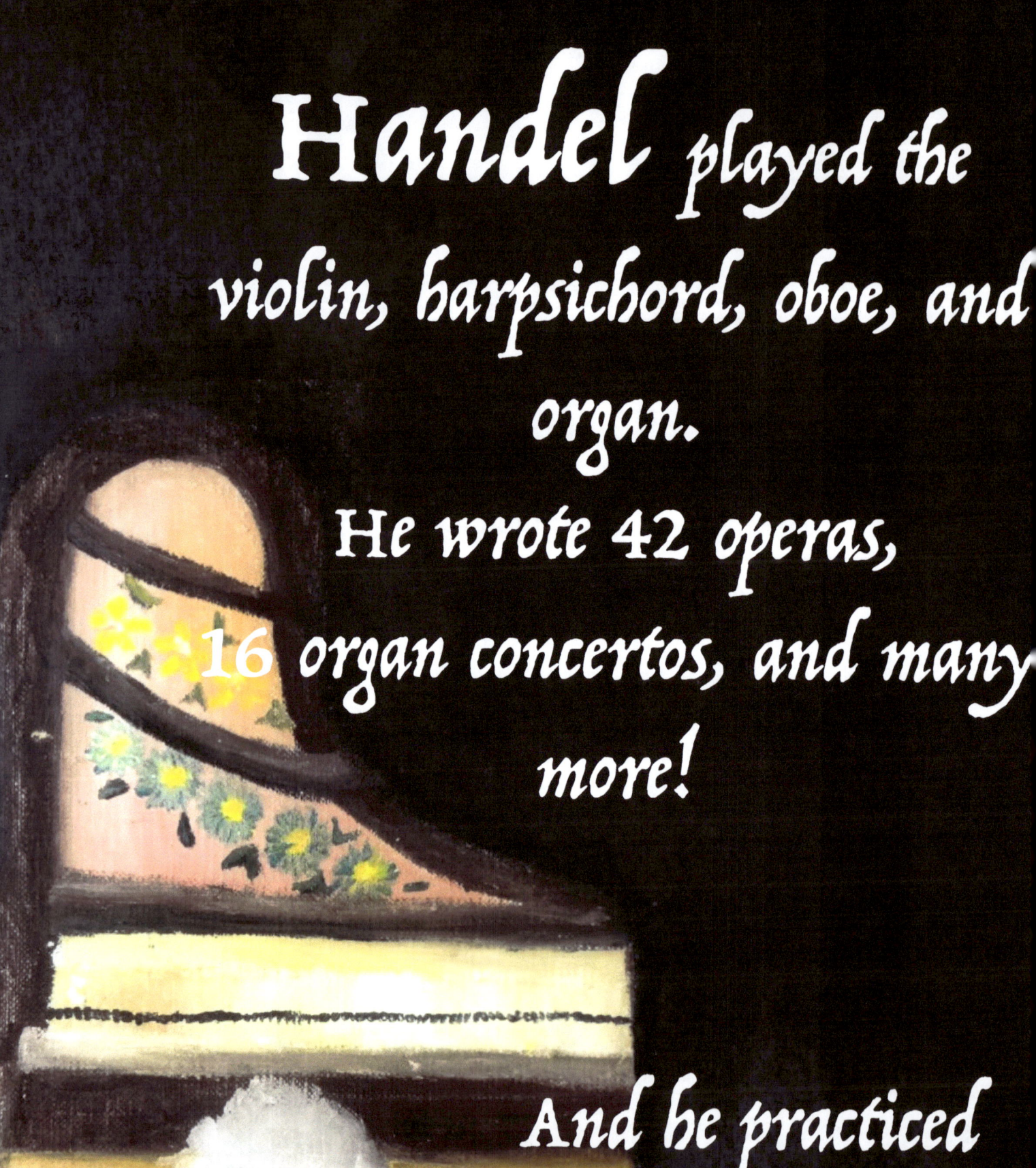

Handel played the violin, harpsichord, oboe, and organ.

He wrote 42 operas, 16 organ concertos, and many more!

And he practiced every day.

They practiced every day because they loved to play.

David looked up and said, "Can you read the art section?"

There were also another group of artists named Poussin, Caravaggio, Rubens, and Rembrandt.

They painted and went to their art lessons.

They used brushes to paint.
They painted dark,
dramatic moments.
They painted dragons,
Greek mythology,
and Christianity into their pieces.

Poussin *painted* "The Companions of Rinaldo" *and many more.* He *painted every day.*

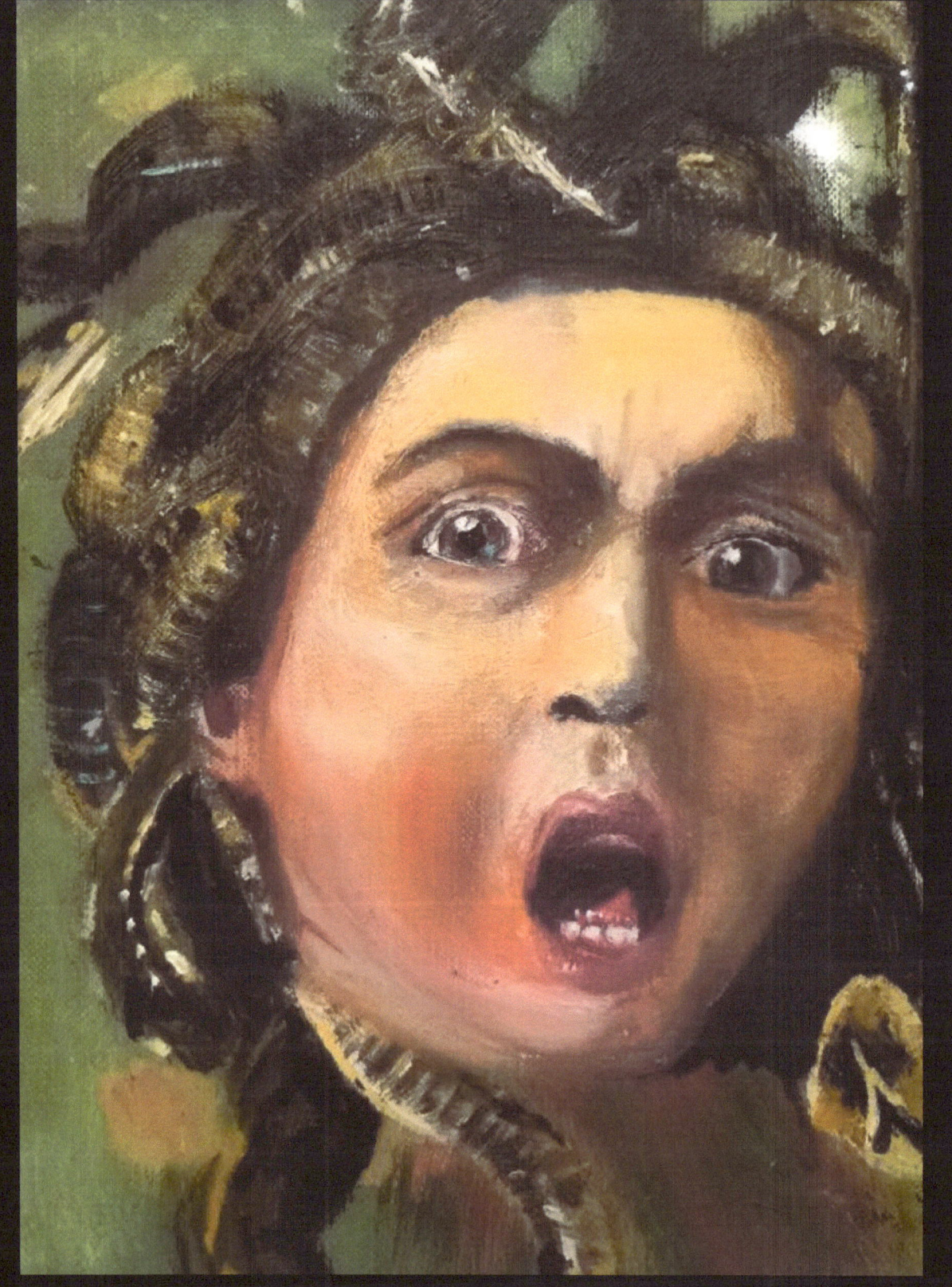

Caravaggio *painted the "Medusa".*
And he painted every day.

Rubens painted "The Raising of the Cross" and many more.
He painted every day.

Rembrandt

painted the "Self-Portrait in a Flat Cap" and many more.
He painted every day.

They all practiced every day because they loved to paint.

"Oh there's even a writing section!" said Isabella. "I like the picture!"

There was also a great Baroque writer. His name was **Miguel de Cervantes.** He wrote the popular Don Quixote.

He used a quill to write his story. He wrote every day.

He practiced every day because he loved to write.

"Wow! I love the quill," said David.
"These musicians, artists, and writer were all greats from the Baroque period," Zoe said and ended her baroque lesson.

Coloring Pages

Copyright © 2015, 2019 Gisel A Costa. All rights reserved.

pearl

Miguel de Cervantes

violin

Copyright © 2015, 2019
Gisel A Costa. All rights reserved.

harpsichord

Copyright © 2015, 2019
Gisel A Costa. All rights reserved.

oboe

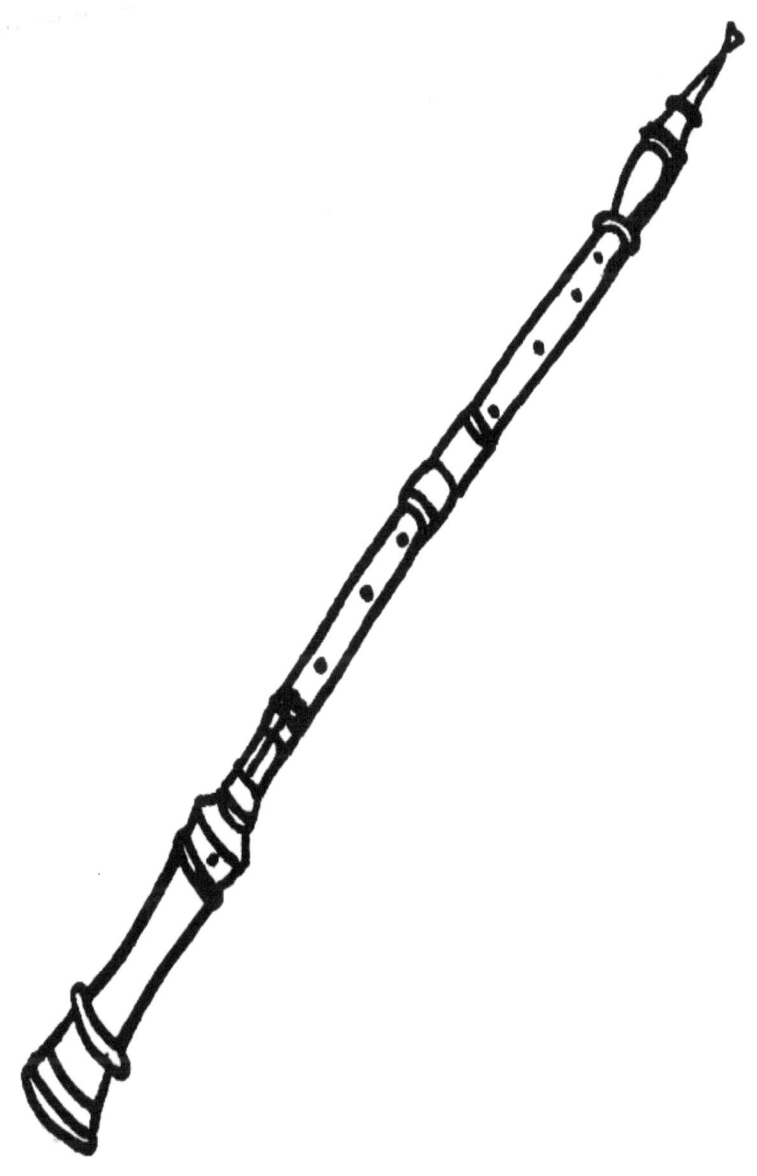

Copyright © 2015, 2019
Gisel A Costa. All rights reserved.

organ

brush

Copyright © 2015, 2019
Gisel A Costa. All rights reserved.

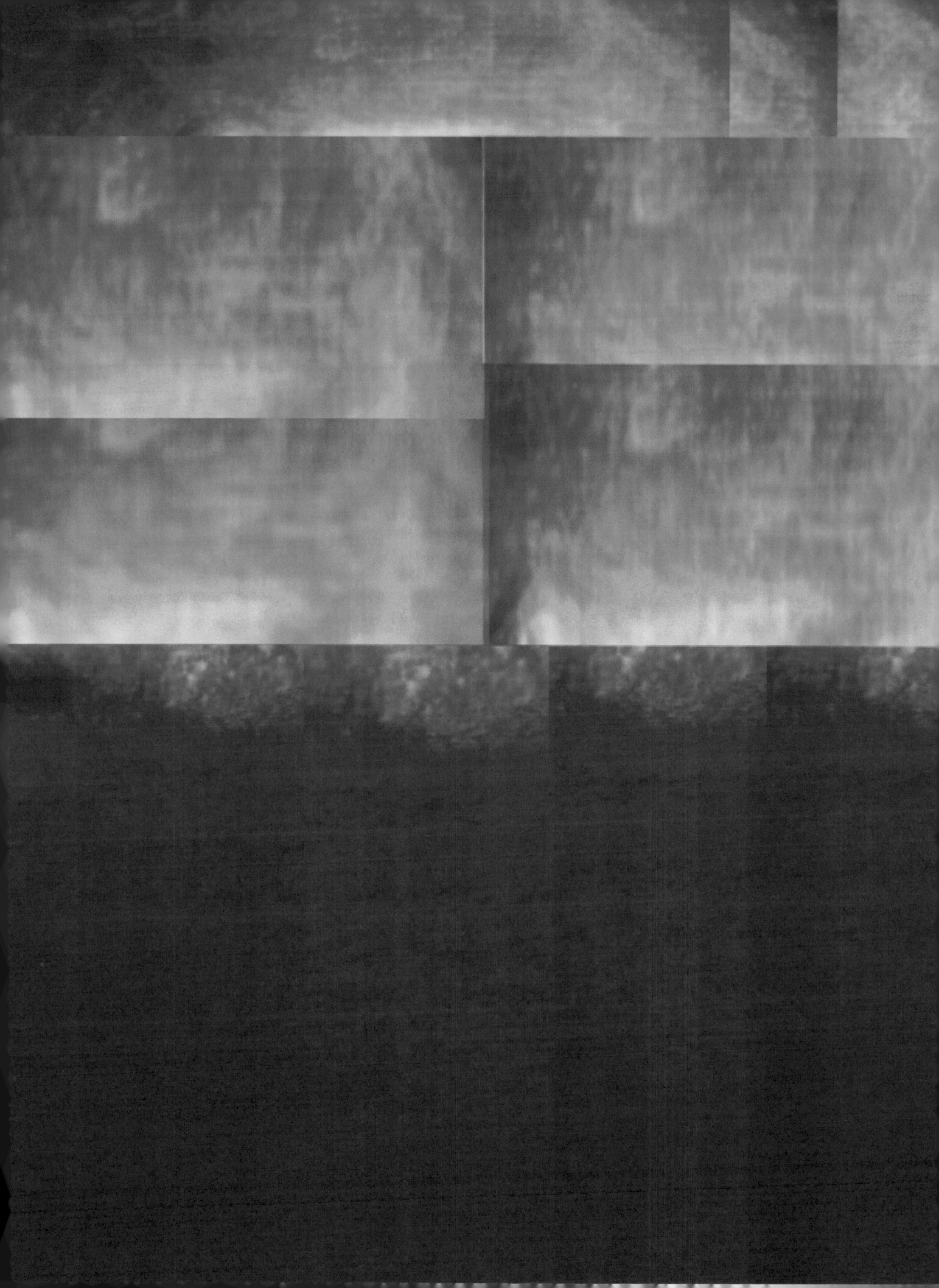

About the Author

Gisel A. Costa is a pianist, composer, instructor, and occasionally tunes pianos. She performed in various venues throughout the tri-state area. She won an Art for Hope Contest when she was 14 and many more awards. She began teaching piano and vocals during her college years. As each lesson went by, she began to fall in love with the aspect of teaching privately and is currently pursuing her passion. It was teaching her students that inspired her to write books to enhance their learning.

SOURCE

"baroque." Vocabulary. Vocabulary, 2017. Web. 1 Feb. 2019.

"The Companions of Rinaldo". Nicolas Poussin, 2017. Web. 1 Feb 2019.

Vanhaleweyk, Guido. "Peter Paul Rubens in Antwerp : Life, Where are his Paintings?" DiscoverFlanders. Web. 2 Feb. 2019.

Wikipedia contributors. "Baroque music." Wikipedia, The Free Encyclopedia. Wikipedia, The Free Encyclopedia, 14 Jan. 2019. Web. 2 Feb. 2019.

Wikipedia contributors. "Baroque violin." Wikipedia, The Free Encyclopedia. Wikipedia, The Free Encyclopedia, 8 Dec. 2018. Web. 2 Feb. 2019.

Wikipedia contributors. "List of paintings by Caravaggio." Wikipedia, The Free Encyclopedia. Wikipedia, The Free Encyclopedia, 17 Jan. 2019. Web. 2 Feb. 2019.

Wikipedia contributors. "Miguel de Cervantes." Wikipedia, The Free Encyclopedia. Wikipedia, The Free Encyclopedia, 26 Jan. 2019. Web. 2 Feb. 2019.

Wikipedia contributors. "Peter Paul Rubens." Wikipedia, The Free Encyclopedia. Wikipedia, The Free Encyclopedia, 29 Jan. 2019. Web. 2 Feb. 2019.

Wikipedia contributors. "Rembrandt." Wikipedia, The Free Encyclopedia. Wikipedia, The Free Encyclopedia, 30 Jan. 2019. Web. 2 Feb. 2019.

About The Eras: The Baroque Story

The Eras: The Baroque Story is a solo project created by Gisel Costa. The pictures and videos on this book and app are painted and assembled by Gisel Costa.

For historical background she relied on various sources, including Wikipedia. She has done some effort by verifying sources to avoid historical errors. If you find a relevant mistake, please let her know.

While she does provide concise relevant information, she has tried to make a visual experience, with pictures and videos for both book and app.

The Baroque Story App is available in App Store

Copyright © 2015, 2019 Gisel A Costa. All rights reserved.

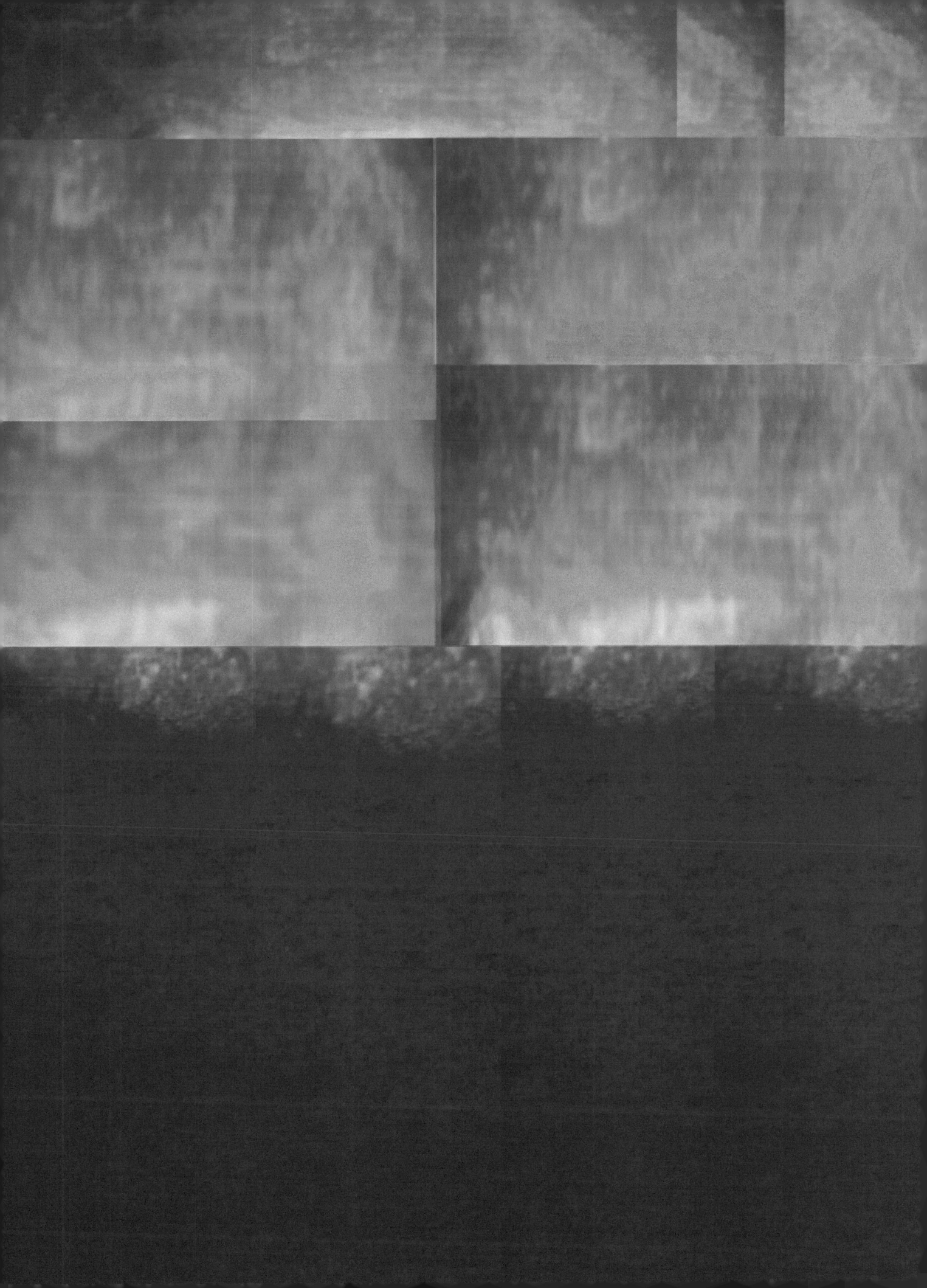

www.ingramcontent.com/pod-product-compliance
Lightning Source LLC
Chambersburg PA
CBHW061359090426
42743CB00002B/76